A GIANT DOSE OF GROSS

Discover the world's most
disgusting animals!

Andy Seed

illustrated by Claire Almon

Quarto is the authority on a wide range of topics.

Quarto educates, entertains and enriches the lives of our readers—enthusiasts and lovers of hands-on living.

www.quartoknows.com

Designer: Clare Barber
Editors: Nancy Dickmann and Emily Pither
Editorial Director: Laura Knowles
Art Director: Susi Martin
Creative Director: Malena Stojic
Publisher: Maxime Boucknooghe

First published in 2019 by QED Publishing,
an imprint of The Quarto Group.
The Old Brewery, 6 Blundell Street,
London, N7 9BH, United Kingdom.
T +44 (0)20 7700 6700
F +44 (0)20 7700 8066
www.QuartoKnows.com

A catalogue record for this book is available from the British Library.

ISBN 978-0-7112-4350-7

Manufactured in Guangdong, China CC072019

9 8 7 6 5 4 3 2 1

Contents

INTRODUCTION

There's one animal on this planet that is truly gross. It often looks awful, makes horrible messes, creates disgusting smells and is loud, rude, annoying, mean, hairy and spotty. Yes, it's the human being!

We've half-wrecked our planet and made life difficult for wildlife on every continent… and yet we have the cheek to label other animals as gross.

But, of course, not every person appears or behaves like this. I'm sure that you are kind, well groomed and free of nasty stinks! However some creatures on Earth are very strange.

So, you can judge for yourself what is gross and what is lovely but I am sure you'll agree that the animals in this book are fascinating. Many of them are important too, keeping nature and the environment in check through their natural actions. So, all in all, gross is good!

POLLUTING PLANES

LOUD MUSIC

NOISY CARS

NOSE PICKING

SMELLY SOCKS

LITTER PILES

SHOCKING SHORTS

4

Why are some animals gross?

Some animals might seem gross to us because of their appearance or their behaviour, but these creatures are like that for a reason. They have adapted to survive and thrive! Here are some examples of animals that are gross for a good reason.

Jellyfish
transparent body
makes it harder for predators to spot

WACKY

Proboscis monkey
giant dangly nose
for attracting a mate and producing louder calls

stinging tentacles
can stun prey or keep away hungry sea creatures

Tick
can latch onto any passing animal without being noticed

sucks blood – a rich and plentiful source of food

big belly to contain the complex stomach needed to digest leaves and other plant material

UGLY

THIRSTY

Vulture
bare head means that feathers won't become matted with blood and bacteria

digestive system contains very strong acid and special bacteria, enabling vultures to eat rotting flesh

YUCKY

Domestic cat
licks bottom to keep it clean and prevent infection

swallows hair during grooming, which means that they sometimes cough up hairballs – this stops their digestive system becoming blocked

UNFUSSY

Tapeworm
gets free food by living off the food that its host eats

Skunk
sprays foul-smelling liquid from its bottom when attacked by a predator. This stinky defence works even against large animals

STINKY

GRISLY

lives inside a host animal (where it is safe from harm) as a parasite

UGLY!: Animals that look gross

The old expression 'beauty is in the eye of the beholder' is just a fancy way of saying that everyone's idea of attractiveness is different. And so is everyone's idea of ugliness! Lots of people might find the creatures in this section ugly or even repulsive and yet their own kind probably see them as rather lovely.

Ugly mammals

Elephant seal

This monster of the sea and land can weigh up to 4 tonnes and measure up to 6 metres in length. The seals can hold their breath for 1½ hours when diving for squid or skate in cold oceans. On land the bulls (males) fight each other for the right to mate with females, using their giant teeth to gash each other. The weird, dangling proboscis helps the bulls to create a deep, croaky roar that will frighten off their rivals.

Baboon

There are five types of baboon, all of which are unloved by most people. These large, intelligent monkeys are found in Africa and Arabia, where they live in groups of up to 50. They eat almost anything, from fruit and farmers' crops to small animals, and are easily recognised by their long faces and brash red bottoms. The female baboon's swollen rear is a sign to the male that she is ready to mate. Surely texting would be easier…

Star-nosed mole

This small, blind North American mammal has to be one of the strangest and most remarkable creatures on the planet. Its weird star-like nose has 25,000 tiny sensory detectors that help it feel its way around and locate food underground. And when it does find a worm or bug to scoff, it's one of the world's fastest eaters, gobbling down prey in less than a quarter of a second!

OTHER UNSIGHTLY MAMMALS

* Ghost bat (a pale bat with a face that's just, well, different)

* Sphynx cat (a hairless puss with a long head and lots of wrinkles)

* Bald uakari (a red-faced monkey that looks like it's suffered terrible sunburn)

* Saiga (an antelope with a humongous hooter)

Naked mole rat

Underneath the deserts of East Africa, in long dark tunnels, live the naked mole rats. These hairless rodents are very strange indeed: they don't drink, they appear to feel no pain and they eat their own poo! They can also live for over 30 years and survive on a quarter of the oxygen that most animals need. But let's just say that they are not the planet's most beautiful animals…

Ugly birds

Shoebill

This is a big bird (up to 1.4 metres tall) with a truly gigantic bill. Found in the swamps of East Africa, it grabs fish, frogs, snakes and even baby crocodiles, using its sharp, high-powered beak to bite off their heads!

What are you looking at?

Great potoo

The great potoo's unusual combo of massive head, huge eyes and wide beak gives it a wonderful cartoon-like appearance. At night it hunts in tropical American forests, with an eerie, wailing croak that has led to many legends. During the day it uses its impressive camouflage skills to impersonate the stump of a tree branch.

Bet you can't spot me!

OTHER UNLOVELY BIRDS

* Muscovy duck (a big fan of red blobby bits around the eyes)
* Long-wattled umbrellabird (a rare jungle inhabitant with an epic dangler!)
* Ocellated turkey (its head appears to be covered in breakfast cereal)
* Marabou stork (looks like it's been sleeping in a hedge)
* Magnificent frigatebird (seabird with a peculiar red throat pouch)

Who cares about looks when there are rotting corpses to snack on?

Andean condor

In the high Andes Mountains of South America soars this enormous vulture, using its tremendous 3-metre wingspan. It can glide for over 30 minutes without flapping while it searches for dead bodies of large animals such as llamas and alpacas.

Ugly fish

Kobudai

Have you ever seen a fish with a chin and a bulging forehead? The female kobudai is small and certainly not gross, but the males are a different story. The proper name of this large Pacific Ocean fish is the Asian sheepshead wrasse and it is famous for being able to change from female to male if it wants to.

I think I'll go back to being a girl!

Goblin shark

Now here's a shark that will give you more nightmares than a great white! This mysterious deep-ocean predator is around 3 metres long. It's not only strange and rare but it also has a curious protruding mouth, enabling it to shoot its jaw forwards to snatch prey. Gruesome!

Blobfish

This unfortunate deep-sea poppet was once voted the world's ugliest animal. It lives about 1 kilometre down in the oceans around Australia, a habitat where its jelly-like flesh and lack of muscle are actually an advantage. The blobfish may be small, pink and gross but with its gloomy expression it's also irresistible!

I've had better days.

OTHER UGLY FISH

* Hammerhead shark (guess what – it's a shark with a head like a hammer)
* Snaggletooth fish (this looks like a sci-fi alien but it's real!)
* Barreleye (its eyes can look out of the top of its transparent head)
* Pacific lamprey (these parasitic fish have special blood-sucking mouths)
* Humpback anglerfish (dark and mean with teeth like daggers)

Warty frogfish

With its comical and colourful appearance, the warty frogfish looks like a harmless little tropical sea creature. But as it tours its coral reef habitat the crafty frogfish waggles a lure: a special spine that looks like a fishing rod with a tasty shrimp on the end. This attracts hungry fish, which are then gobbled up by the warty hunter.

Here, fishy fishy fishy!

Ugly reptiles and amphibians

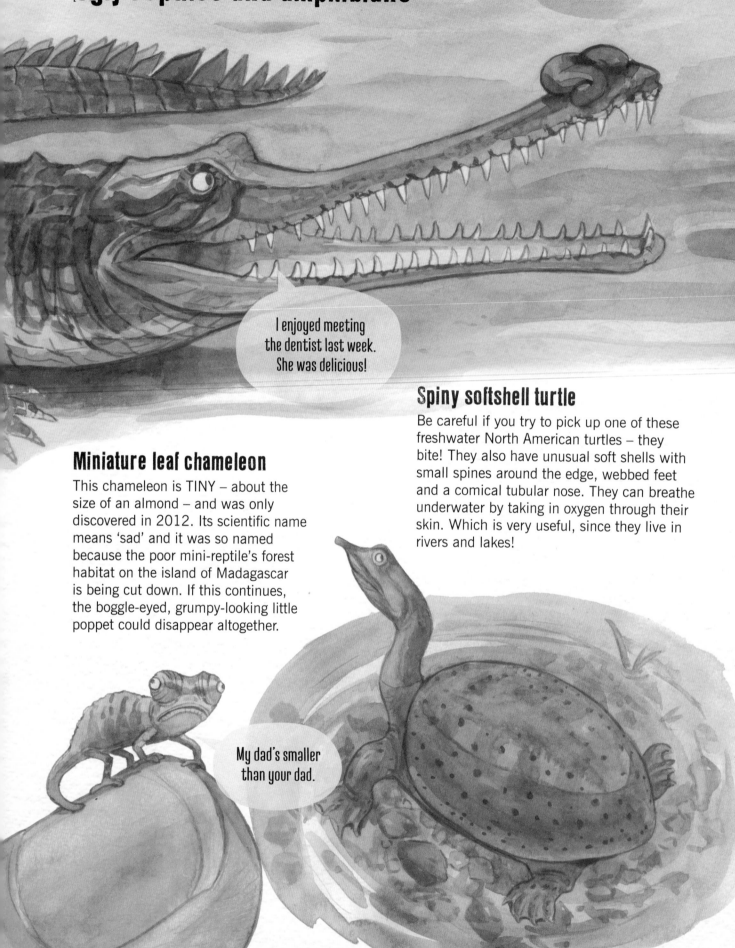

I enjoyed meeting the dentist last week. She was delicious!

Miniature leaf chameleon

This chameleon is TINY – about the size of an almond – and was only discovered in 2012. Its scientific name means 'sad' and it was so named because the poor mini-reptile's forest habitat on the island of Madagascar is being cut down. If this continues, the boggle-eyed, grumpy-looking little poppet could disappear altogether.

My dad's smaller than your dad.

Spiny softshell turtle

Be careful if you try to pick up one of these freshwater North American turtles – they bite! They also have unusual soft shells with small spines around the edge, webbed feet and a comical tubular nose. They can breathe underwater by taking in oxygen through their skin. Which is very useful, since they live in rivers and lakes!

Gharial

These huge crocodiles use their slender snouts (armed with 110 teeth) to grab fish from rivers. The male gharial can grow up to 6 metres long and has a strange 'nose bulb', which it uses to call to a mate and to blow bubbles!

Burp!

Amazonian horned frog

Here's another grumpy-faced beast, this time found in the rainforests of South America. It's a big amphibian with a mouth over 1½ times wider than its body length. It uses this colossal gob to gulp down any passing frog or small animal unlucky enough to be ambushed. Just don't get too close…

Surinam toad

This South American swamp-dweller has a peculiar flat body that looks like it's been trodden on by a hippo. It also has no tongue and, to make it really interesting, the toad's eggs develop on the female's BACK and its babies break out through her skin to be born. Gross!

Ugly invertebrates
False garden mantis

Mantids are large hunting insects famed for eating anything they can catch. The false garden mantis lives in Australia where it hides among leaves, looking out for prey. Its bulgy eyes give it excellent vision, and its powerful spiny forelegs are built for springing onto passing victims. Some types of mantids also have eyes that change colour at night, often from green to red or purple.

Let us prey.

Star spider

The star spider's abdomen looks like a six-pointed star with many colour variations. It is found across the Americas and nearby islands, where it makes large webs. The unlucky insects caught in the webs have their juices sucked out by the hungry spider.

I'm a star – a death star!

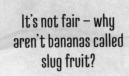

It's not fair – why aren't bananas called slug fruit?

Banana slug

This is a monster of a slug, growing up to 25 centimetres long. And yes, it really does look like a banana! It's found in North America, where it moves so slowly that it would take 4 days to go one kilometre. The banana slug is always on the lookout for dead plant material and animal poo to feed on. But here's an even grosser fact: some people eat banana slugs (once they've removed the unpleasant slime).

Yeti crab

This hairy-armed crustacean was only discovered in 2005, deep in the Pacific Ocean. It is small, has no eyes and has limbs covered with strange bristles called setae. The crabs live near hydrothermal vents (underwater volcanic holes that gush out extra-hot water) and appear to eat bacteria that grow on their bodies… very nice!

Sea pig

At the bottom of the deep oceans, up to 5 kilometres down, live strange pink wobbly creatures. They are about the size of large potatoes and they gather in groups of hundreds to sift through the seabed mud. These are sea pigs and they are searching for food, especially their favourite snack: whale corpses.

OTHER GROSS INVERTEBRATES? YOU DECIDE!

Want more grossness? Check out these animals and decide if they deserve a place in the 'Ugliest Invertebrates' hall of fame.

* Bobbit worm
* Giraffe weevil
* Japanese spider crab
* Sea slug
* Giant millipede

Any ice cream for you? Today's flavours are raspberry and beaver butt.

YUCKY!: Animals that do gross things

We've already decided that human beings, with our burps, farts, spitting, snot-picking and worse, are the yuckiest animal of all. But what about other creatures? Here are some examples of behaviours found in nature that most people consider to be gross. Like always, however, there are good reasons for each one.

Nice to sniff you

Beaver

These famous dam-building mammals have a special gland in their bottom that produces a yellowy-brown sticky substance called castoreum. Beavers sniff castoreum as a way of picking up information. Amazingly, castoreum smells like vanilla and has been used in the past to flavour ice cream and puddings!

Dog

According to scientists who know these things, a dog's nose is over 10,000 times better at detecting smells than a human's. Dogs communicate with each other through special chemicals released from glands in their bum, so when they sniff each other's backside they're actually having a kind of pongy chat!

I wonder what's in the news today ...

Howler monkey

These noisy primates are found across Central America. Males have been observed to pee on their hands and then rub them over their body. This is thought to make them more attractive to females seeking a mate. Another smelly habit howler monkeys have is to drop wee and poo from the trees on humans who disturb them. You have been warned!

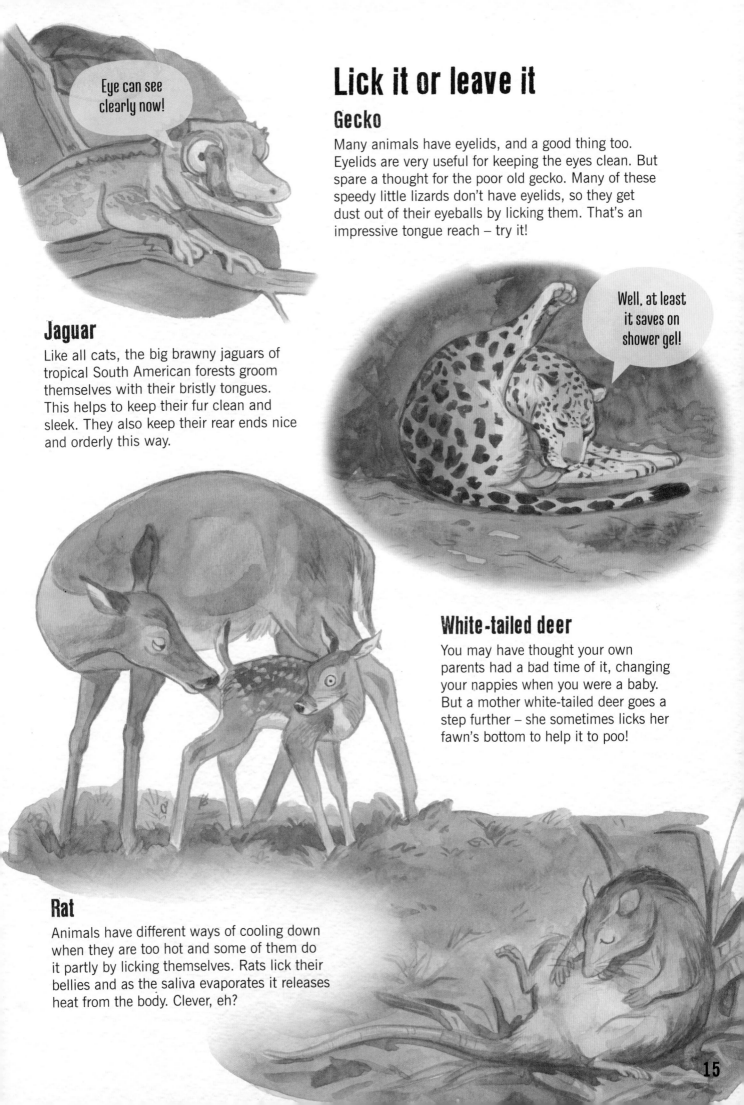

Eye can see clearly now!

Lick it or leave it

Gecko

Many animals have eyelids, and a good thing too. Eyelids are very useful for keeping the eyes clean. But spare a thought for the poor old gecko. Many of these speedy little lizards don't have eyelids, so they get dust out of their eyeballs by licking them. That's an impressive tongue reach – try it!

Well, at least it saves on shower gel!

Jaguar

Like all cats, the big brawny jaguars of tropical South American forests groom themselves with their bristly tongues. This helps to keep their fur clean and sleek. They also keep their rear ends nice and orderly this way.

White-tailed deer

You may have thought your own parents had a bad time of it, changing your nappies when you were a baby. But a mother white-tailed deer goes a step further – she sometimes licks her fawn's bottom to help it to poo!

Rat

Animals have different ways of cooling down when they are too hot and some of them do it partly by licking themselves. Rats lick their bellies and as the saliva evaporates it releases heat from the body. Clever, eh?

Don't come too close!

European roller

This rare and stunning bird is the size of a crow but has vibrant turquoise-blue feathers. It also has chicks who know how to discourage predators who approach their nest. Baby rollers vomit a stinky orange liquid over themselves, putting the attacker right off its dinner. Sick does the trick!

Camel

The camel is one of the champion spitters of the animal world. Camel spit is not just saliva, though – it's much more gross than that! When feeling threatened, a camel can bring up part of the contents of its stomach and then fire this pongy puke mixture out of its mouth at annoying people or perhaps hungry wolves. So, be nice to camels!

Regal horned lizard

This small, slow desert-dweller cannot outrun predators, so it uses camouflage as a defence. But if that doesn't work, the lizard has another trick up its sleeve. It can raise the blood pressure around its eyes until the blood vessels burst, sending a jet of dark blood shooting out from its eye. That has to be high on the gross-o-meter!

Don't try this at home!

16

Fieldfare

Sometimes this bird's chicks are attacked in their nest by big ravens looking for a meal. Parent fieldfares are too small to fight the raven so they fly above it, dive-bombing it with poo. The sticky fieldfare faeces can goo up the wings of the raven, making flight difficult. Perhaps this defence isn't so surprising in a bird with the scientific name *Turdus pilaris*!

Bum's away!

Colorado potato beetle

This stripy insect has larvae (young) with a disgusting but clever way of keeping predators at bay. First, they eat a plant called bittersweet nightshade, which is full of nasty toxins. Next, the crafty maggots coat themselves in their own poisonous poo. It's stinky, but it works!

Can you smell something nasty?

Yes, it's those roses over there!

MORE YUCKY DEFENCES

* Bombardier beetles spray very hot, dangerous chemicals out of their rear ends.

* Dwarf sperm whales squirt stinky brown ink into the water to blind sharks.

* Malaysian exploding ants burst open their abdomens and release harmful yellow goo.

* Garden dormice can detach their tails if grabbed by an attacker.

Sea cucumber

Sea cucumbers, who live on the ocean floor, are some of the strangest animals on the planet. They have no brains, but they do have a spectacularly yucky defence to use against predators. If attacked they can eject their guts out of their bottoms. These toxic tubes can tangle up and even kill fish that get too close. They then quickly grow new innards. Nice!

I've got a gut feeling this will work.

Dead clever!

Nursery web spider

Dead things are often gross. Lifeless bodies quickly decompose (rot), giving off a gross smell. They are invaded by maggots and harmful bacteria, making them unpleasant to eat for many animals. A good example is the male nursery web spider, who sometimes pretends to be dead to stop a female from eating him!

Erk. I'd better arrange a funeral!

Opossum

Imagine the scene: a large, hungry bobcat is on the prowl, looking for a fresh meal. It sees a small mammal scuttling down from a tree and corners the defenceless animal, which gives a growl. But as the hunter is about to pounce, the animal lies stiff, its mouth foaming and its body reeking of rotting flesh. The bobcat pokes it, sniffs it and retreats in disgust. When all is clear the animal stands up, unharmed. This is the opossum.

OPOSSUM FACTS

* Opossums are marsupials found in North and South America.
* When attacked they do not actually 'play dead' – their reaction is more like fainting.
* They give off the scent of decay from a gland in their bottom.
* Opossums can lie still with eyes half-closed and tongue sticking out for hours.

18

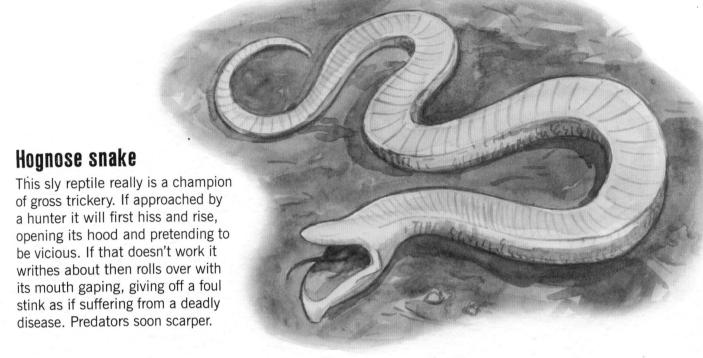

Hognose snake

This sly reptile really is a champion of gross trickery. If approached by a hunter it will first hiss and rise, opening its hood and pretending to be vicious. If that doesn't work it writhes about then rolls over with its mouth gaping, giving off a foul stink as if suffering from a deadly disease. Predators soon scarper.

Duck

Foxes love nothing better for dinner than a juicy wild duck. But when captured in a fox's mouth, many species of duck will go limp and silent, craftily playing dead. The fox, thinking that the job is done, will often put down the bird, only for it to spring up and flap away when the fox isn't looking. In one study by scientists, more than half of ducks captured managed to escape this way!

Ssssh, they think we've croaked it!

Missionary leaf litter frog

This little amphibian has one of the best fake corpses in the animal kingdom: lying on its back still as stone, limbs out and eyes closed. Not gross but gifted!

Waste disposal and more

Hairball heaving

Pet cats sometimes cough up small hairballs, the result of them swallowing fur while grooming by licking. Big cats occasionally do this too, but their hairballs are much larger! A lion will sometimes vomit a bundle the size of a bread roll. One tiger in a US zoo had a hairball weighing nearly 2 kilograms!

For my next birthday present, I'd like a comb!

I don't feel well...

Humans do it, dogs and cats do it and many wild animals do it too. Vomiting is usually a sign that the body wants to get rid of something unwelcome that has been swallowed. Some animals, such as seabirds, bring up partly digested food to feed their young. Snakes sometimes regurgitate a swallowed animal because they are stressed, perhaps by another predator.

Pellet puking

Owls and many other birds of prey swallow mice and other small animals whole. They cannot digest bones, feathers or fur, so these parts are held in a special stomach called the gizzard. Eventually, all of the non-digestible bits are compressed together and the owl coughs up a pellet. Gulls, jackdaws, crows, storks and herons produce these small stinky parcels too.

SICK FACTS

* Horses, rabbits and rats cannot vomit.

* Even dinosaurs puked! A fossilised barf 160 million years old has been found in the UK.

* Some sharks can literally puke their guts out. They push their stomach through their mouth to eject its contents.

* Many flies spew on their food before eating it.

* Whale vomit can be valuable! Sperm whales throw up a rare waxy substance called ambergris, which is sometimes used to make expensive perfumes.

Wee warnings

As tigers walk around their hunting territories, they spray urine on rocks and trees and the ground. They do this scent-marking as a sign to other tigers to keep away. Neighbouring rivals who smell the chemicals in the pee know that the territory is taken. Many other animals including wolves, pandas and mice scent mark in this way.

My territory keeps moving ever since I peed on that badger.

On a roll

Warthogs and many other animals love rolling around in gluey mud. It can help remove skin parasites and cool them down, and it also works as a sunscreen. Dogs often roll in cow or fox poo and other really pongy substances. But hyenas are champions of grossness – they love to roll around in their own vomit.

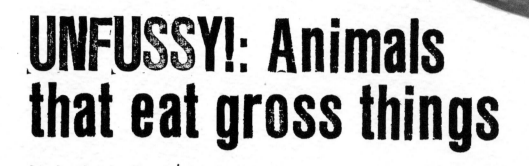

UNFUSSY!: Animals that eat gross things

Human beings have shops, cafes, takeaways and stalls that sell sandwiches and snacks. Wild animals don't have any of these things. They have to go and find their food, every day. Some eat whatever they can find and if they are predators, they grab and gobble their prey before it escapes. It might appear gross to us but it's all about staying alive!

Fresh food
Burmese python

These monster snakes, which grow up to 4 metres long, are natives of southeast Asia but many people in the USA keep them as pets. Some of these pythons have escaped and bred in the wild, especially in the swamps of Florida. Like other snakes, they swallow their prey whole, and will happily gulp down small deer and even young alligators.

It's very dark in here – anyone got a torch?

Don't worry, you'll only be one foot shorter.

Nile crocodile

This fearsome beast grows up to 5 metres long and has the most powerful bite in the world. It will attack almost anything that comes into the water, including large zebras and wildebeest. The croc drags its victim underwater to drown it, then rips off big chunks of flesh by twisting its body violently. Just be careful where you paddle…

African bullfrog

This bulky amphibian is not a fussy eater, and it also likes a quick dinner. The bullfrog prefers to swallow its victims whole, using its sharp teeth to get a good grip first. Items on the bullfrog's lunch menu include rats, small birds and snakes.

Hurry up, my dessert's going cold!

Pelican

Pelicans usually eat fish, but in 2010, tourists in St James's Park in London watched as a large pelican grabbed a nearby pigeon and attempted to swallow it. The smaller bird fought for fifteen minutes in the pelican's throat pouch before it was finally guzzled.

Orca

Orcas are huge, powerful, intelligent and deadly. They prowl the seas in gangs and can swallow seal pups whole, sometimes grabbing them off beaches. They also like to dine on sea lions, dolphins, small whales and even sharks!

Hey, I can see the lighthouse from here.

I WILL SURVIVE!

Occasionally, animals are swallowed but come out of it alive...

* In 2012, stunned scientists watched a small snake wriggling out of a toad's bottom. The snake had been eaten earlier and had passed right through the toad's digestive system.

* Some types of snail eaten by birds are pooed out alive.

* Rough-skinned newts are small but highly toxic creatures. They are sometimes swallowed by big frogs, which die within minutes, allowing the newts to crawl out of their mouth, unharmed.

You eat what?!

Oxpecker

Quick makeover, madam? Oxpeckers are African birds that spend their time perched on the backs of large mammals such as zebras, cattle, rhinos, hippos and giraffes. They eat parasites such as insects and biting ticks, which live off these big beasts. However, the oxpecker also likes a bit of variety now and again and so will happily nibble away at their hosts' blood, mucus, dandruff and earwax too!

Bearded vulture

Bearded vultures are scavengers who even eat bones. They drop them onto rocks from the air to smash them then digest the pieces with their extra-strong gut acid.

Oh no, I've just hit David Attenborough!

Spotted hyena

Spotted hyenas are hunters who just hate to see any part of a victim go to waste. They will gobble down hooves, eyes, brains, bones, hair, horns and even teeth. Gross, maybe, but it does help prevent the spread of disease.

Komodo dragon

Komodo dragons are giant lizards that eat most of whatever animal they can capture. They even chow down on the intestines – once they've shaken out any poo, of course. They don't want to be called disgusting!

Mite

This may come as a shock, but you have a whole host of small creatures living on your face. These mites are too small to see, partly because they are only a third of a millimetre long, but mainly because they stay buried in small pores around hairs and eyelashes. The mites eat the oily substances made by our skin but they are not usually harmful. Feeling itchy?

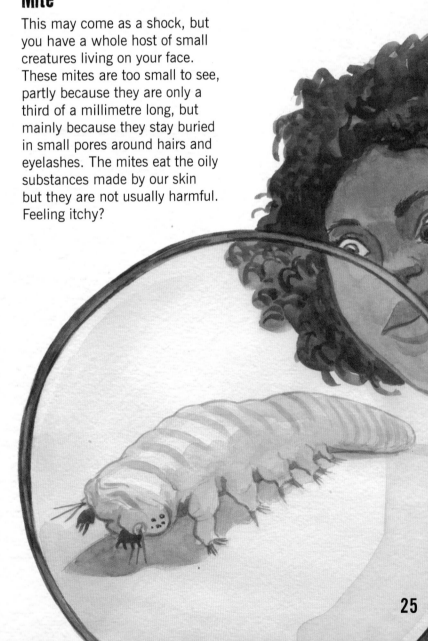

DUNG DINERS

A surprising number of animals eat poo, including these:

* Dung beetles love other animals' plops. They bury them, live in them and enjoy chomping them, too. These tiny poo patrol heroes help counter climate change by reducing the problem gases that cow poos give off.

* Guinea pigs and rabbits recycle their poos by eating them to get more goodness.

* Chimpanzees look through their turds for half-digested items to snack on.

* Panda cubs eat their parents' faeces. Think about that before complaining about what's for dinner!

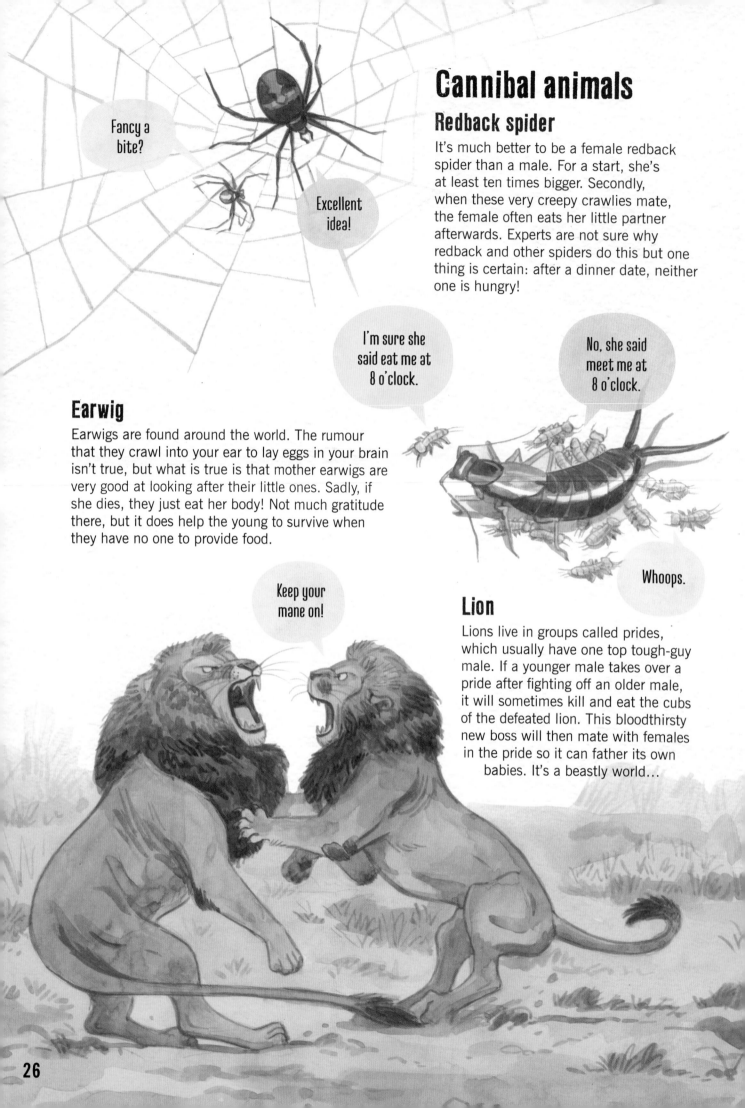

Fancy a bite?

Excellent idea!

Cannibal animals

Redback spider

It's much better to be a female redback spider than a male. For a start, she's at least ten times bigger. Secondly, when these very creepy crawlies mate, the female often eats her little partner afterwards. Experts are not sure why redback and other spiders do this but one thing is certain: after a dinner date, neither one is hungry!

I'm sure she said eat me at 8 o'clock.

No, she said meet me at 8 o'clock.

Earwig

Earwigs are found around the world. The rumour that they crawl into your ear to lay eggs in your brain isn't true, but what is true is that mother earwigs are very good at looking after their little ones. Sadly, if she dies, they just eat her body! Not much gratitude there, but it does help the young to survive when they have no one to provide food.

Whoops.

Keep your mane on!

Lion

Lions live in groups called prides, which usually have one top tough-guy male. If a younger male takes over a pride after fighting off an older male, it will sometimes kill and eat the cubs of the defeated lion. This bloodthirsty new boss will then mate with females in the pride so it can father its own babies. It's a beastly world…

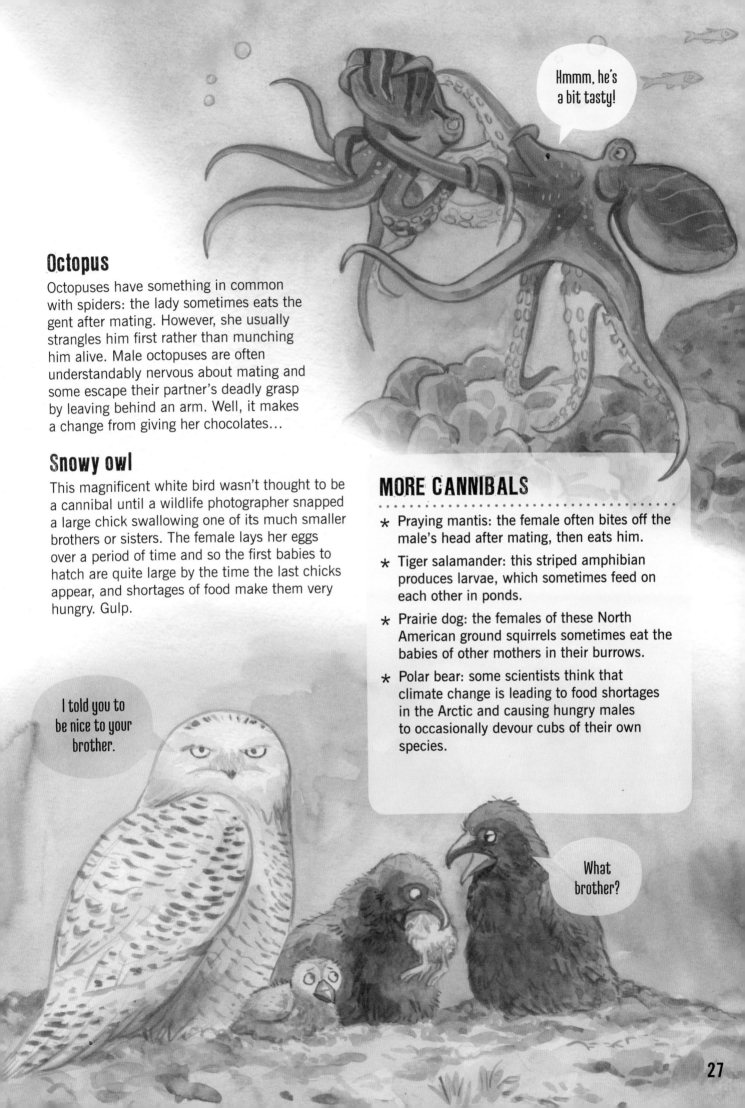

Octopus

Octopuses have something in common with spiders: the lady sometimes eats the gent after mating. However, she usually strangles him first rather than munching him alive. Male octopuses are often understandably nervous about mating and some escape their partner's deadly grasp by leaving behind an arm. Well, it makes a change from giving her chocolates…

Snowy owl

This magnificent white bird wasn't thought to be a cannibal until a wildlife photographer snapped a large chick swallowing one of its much smaller brothers or sisters. The female lays her eggs over a period of time and so the first babies to hatch are quite large by the time the last chicks appear, and shortages of food make them very hungry. Gulp.

MORE CANNIBALS

* Praying mantis: the female often bites off the male's head after mating, then eats him.

* Tiger salamander: this striped amphibian produces larvae, which sometimes feed on each other in ponds.

* Prairie dog: the females of these North American ground squirrels sometimes eat the babies of other mothers in their burrows.

* Polar bear: some scientists think that climate change is leading to food shortages in the Arctic and causing hungry males to occasionally devour cubs of their own species.

Carrion dining

Blowfly

These very common flies lay their eggs on the carcasses of dead creatures. The eggs hatch into larvae, which are often called maggots. They eat the decaying flesh. Maggots also feed on the wounds of injured animals such as cattle and sheep.

Sexton beetle

There are many types of burying beetle, including the sexton beetle, which buries the bodies of dead birds and mice before feeding on their corpses.

Poor thing, let's give it a decent burial.

Yeah, and then eat it.

Tasmanian devil

On the Australian island of Tasmania lurks the world's largest carnivorous marsupial. It has a famously growly temper and will fight other Tasmanian devils to feast on roadkill, such as the bodies of dead kangaroos. These unfussy eaters sometimes pull out an animal's intestines and then crawl into the body cavity to munch through meat, bones and even fur.

Finish that eyeball or you're not having any pudding!

Other curious eaters

Red garra

Eat my feet! These tiny red garra fish from Asia are used in health treatments because they will nibble away the dead skin on people's feet. Tasty! As a result they are known as doctor fish, even though they don't actually cure anything.

Apart from tasting of sweaty socks, it's delicious.

Easy, squeezy!

Snake

The largest snakes in the world are pythons, boas and anacondas. These giant reptiles squeeze their victims to death and then swallow them whole. However, some people keep them indoors as pets and this leads them to sometimes gulp down strange objects. Golf balls, soft toys and even blankets have all been found inside snakes.

Ostrich

The world's largest bird, the ostrich, eats mainly grass, leaves and seeds with maybe the odd flower. But the poor creature has no teeth to chew them up! Its solution is to swallow up to a kilogram of stones, which help to grind up food in one of its three stomachs.

THIRSTY!: Animals that drink blood

While we may not appreciate small creatures climbing onto our skin, making a hole and then having a merry slurp of our most precious bodily fluid, we should admire their courage. After all, they are much smaller than us! But blood is a plentiful source of food, rich in protein and vitamins, so it's worth the risk for them to take a swig.

Biting bloodsuckers
Horsefly

Most biting insects are quite small, but the horsefly is big. It has to be, if it wants to bite through the thick, tough skin of cows and horses! Unluckily for us, horseflies like human blood too. The female has a pair of serrated cutters on her mouth that she uses to saw into skin, sometimes even through clothing!

Head louse

Head lice strike fear into many people, probably because they live permanently on human heads, rather than just visiting occasionally to eat. These small wingless insects are 2–3 millimetres long. They cling on to hairs using special claws and bite four or five times a day to feed on blood. The females lay eggs, which attach to strands of hair.

This new hairstyle is really lousy.

Highland midge

This tiny but bloodthirsty little beastie is the sworn enemy of many visitors to Scotland and Scandinavia during the summer months. They gather in swarms like small clouds, often near water, and can detect human breath up to 200 metres away. Like other biting insects, they use a special substance to prevent blood from clotting when they bite.

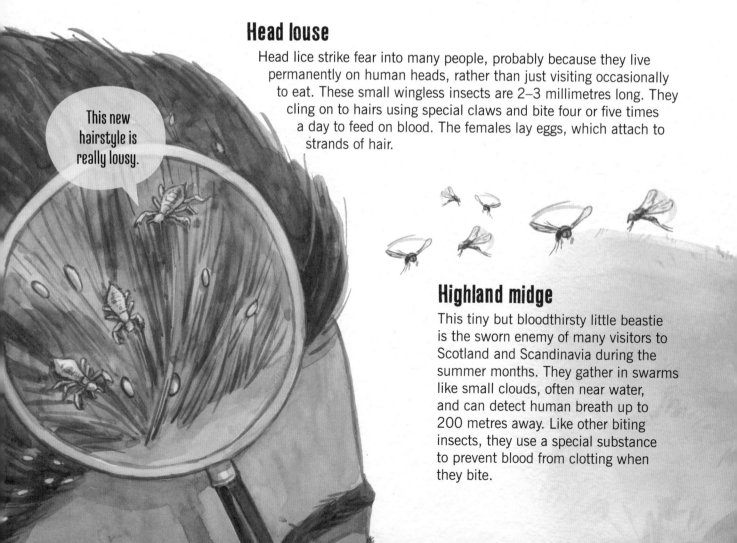

Assassin bug

Assassin bugs are a large group of insects found in hot countries around the world. Some have a sharp 'beak', which they use to pierce the bodies of their prey (mostly insects and spiders). They inject victims with a venom that turns their insides to liquid. The assassin bug then sucks out the liquid for its lunch. Gross but efficient!

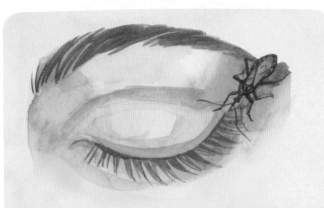

GIVE US A KISS!

One type of assassin bug is known as a kissing bug because it often bites people around the mouth while they sleep. It also sucks blood from around the eyes and will nibble dogs as well as humans. Despite the name, these bites are not usually dangerous – but they are certainly gross!

Sandfly

The different types of sandfly all live around sandy areas like beaches, and they are very keen to bite people whenever possible. In New Zealand there is a very common small sandfly known as a blackfly, which patrols the country's coast. Its bites cause itchy rashes on sunbathers and tourists. Scientists have recorded over 1000 bites an hour in the worst affected areas.

ANIMALS THAT BITE HUMANS BUT DON'T DRINK BLOOD

* Ants
* Spiders
* Rats
* Snakes
* Monkeys
* Pigs

Vampires!

Vampire bat

In the dead of night in South and Central America, dark shapes flutter out of caves, seeking sleeping birds and mammals. They land, walk silently, and bite their victim with needle-sharp teeth. These are vampire bats. They lap up blood from the wound like a cat laps milk, leaving the unknowing victim still asleep.

COME ON, THOSE ARE GROSS!

OK, yes, they do drink blood without asking, but they are small, painless biters, that avoid killing, and are also kind creatures: a full bat will share its meal with hungry bats back in the roost (admittedly, that involves a bit of gory sicking up…).

Yum, fangs for that!

JUICY VAMPIRE BAT FACTS

Common vampire bats…

* Have heat-seeking noses for locating blood vessels on animals.

* Are the only bats that can run.

* Can double in weight when feeding.

* Have a substance called draculin in their spit that stops blood clotting.

* Dine on cattle, pigs, chickens, horses, sea lions, snakes and, occasionally, humans!

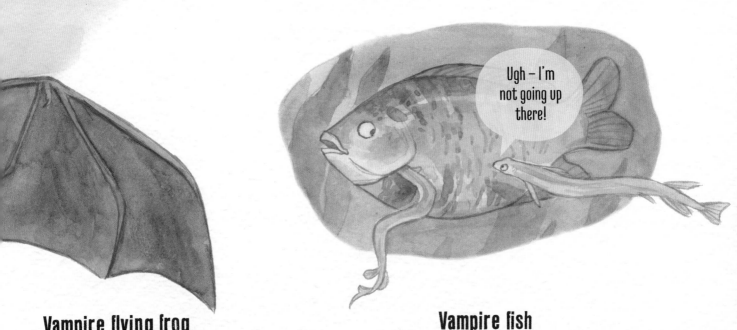

Vampire flying frog

This little croaker was only discovered in 2008 in the high cloud forests of Vietnam. To avoid predators, it lays its eggs in foam nests near water-filled holes in trees. When they hatch, the tadpoles have no food so their mum lays more eggs in the water. The tadpoles hook these out using tiny curved fangs and eat them!

Vampire fish

A tiny Amazon catfish called the candiru has a fearsome reputation for wriggling into holes, such as the gills of big fish, and slurping blood. It has special spikes to latch on while feeding. Legend says that this mini-vampire can swim into painful places in people who are enjoying a quiet wee in the river. But – thankfully! – there is no evidence to support this.

Vampire finch

This harmless-looking small bird helps the large blue-footed booby (a seabird) by removing insects from its feathers. However, it also sometimes pecks through the skin and has a sneaky feed on the booby's blood. This might seem gross to us, but the booby doesn't seem to mind!

Dangerous visitors

Tsetse fly

Blood-sucking tsetse flies are found across Africa and are much feared by people there because they spread a deadly disease called sleeping sickness. They also bite animals, passing on a similar disease called nagana. The good news is that there are now cures for these illnesses.

Hmmm, this guy tastes like chicken.

Ticks

Ticks are tiny creatures that look like spiders with short legs and teardrop-shaped bodies. They love to bite humans and other mammals to feed on their blood. Sometimes they bury their whole head in the skin as they slurp! Most tick bites are harmless and not even painful but some ticks pass on diseases, such as typhus, which are no fun at all.

Mosquito

Mosquitoes are small flies found all over the world but especially in hot countries. They fly very slowly, at less than 2 miles per hour. They may be slow, but these hungry insects exist in mind-boggling numbers and they carry more disease around the planet than any other creature. Mozzies use the blood they drink to help their eggs develop.

ROTTEN RABIES

Foxes, raccoons and bats are not normally dangerous to people, but in some parts of the world they may be carrying a gruesome disease: rabies. Dogs and cats can also carry rabies and a bite from an infected animal can pass it onto humans. Rabies can be treated if it is caught early, but if untreated it's fatal. So really it's best avoided!

OTHER ANIMALS THAT CAN CARRY RABIES

* Skunks
* Coyotes
* Jackals
* Cows
* Mongooses

Selected biters

Flea

Fleas want your blood! These very small, wingless insects jump about looking for animals to bite. There are bird fleas, cat fleas, dog fleas and even armadillo fleas! There are human fleas too, which cause really itchy, red, swollen bite marks. Fortunately, these little blighters are not as common as they once were. Phew!

How did I get my name? When dogs see me coming, they flea!

FLEA FACTS

* Fleas can jump over 50 times their body length.

* Fleas are amazingly strong for their size and were once used to pull miniature carriages in 'flea circuses' for entertainment.

* The Black Death, a plague that killed a large proportion of Europe's population in the 1300s, was partly spread by fleas.

* The larvae of fleas eat the poo of adult fleas.

Leech

Worms are not usually predators, but the leech is different. These strange, slug-like bloodsuckers were once put on the skin of sick people. Doctors thought that having too much blood was making them ill – and leeches could take care of that little problem! Some hospitals still use leeches today to help keep blood flowing during surgery.

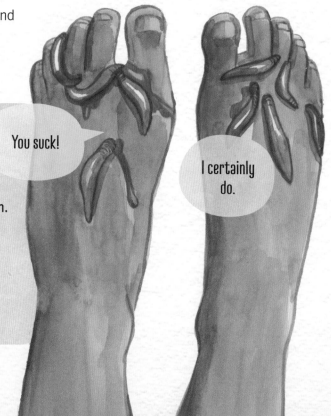

You suck!

I certainly do.

LEECH FACTS

* Many leeches have sharp teeth.
* Leech bites are not painful because they inject special anaesthetic substances into the skin.
* Some types of leech can grow up to 20 centimetres long.
* A leech that has consumed blood does not need to feed again for several months.

Bedbug

These sneaky brown insects are about 5 millimetres long and often hide around beds, waiting to bite sleeping people at night. The bites cause an itchy rash but at least bedbugs do not carry diseases – so they're annoying rather than deadly! They have skin-sawing mouthparts and usually feast on the face, neck or arms.

Night night, hope the bedbugs do bite!

BEDBUG FACTS

* Bedbugs can be found in hotels and even aircraft that are not cleaned carefully.
* They often hide in cracks in walls.
* Bedbugs feed on blood every 5–7 days.
* They often make a line of bite marks on the skin.

Sea lamprey

Sea lampreys are fish that have a special sucking mouth armed with vicious teeth. They use this to attach themselves to larger fish to suck their blood. The victim sometimes dies from blood loss or infection! But before you refuse to swim in the sea, there's one fact you should know – this parasite doesn't nosh on humans.

SEA LAMPREY FACTS

* Sea lampreys sometimes attach themselves to sharks.
* They often stay attached to a victim for up to a year.
* Females produce up to 170,000 eggs.
* Sea lampreys swim up rivers to spawn.

GRISLY!: Animals that live in other animals

. . . .

If you're a small creature looking for a home, what could be better than somewhere warm and soft, with a ready supply of free food? It sounds perfect, and that is why so many living things live on or in the bodies of others. These (mainly unwanted) visitors love nothing better than to suck their host's blood, steal their food – and even control their mind.

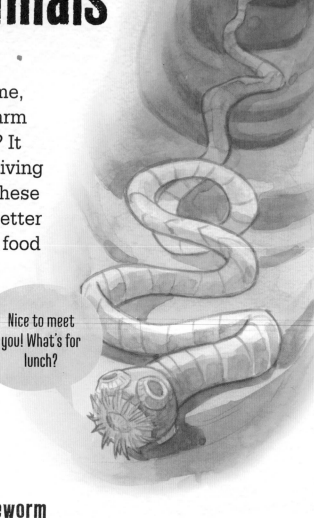

Nice to meet you! What's for lunch?

The world of parasites

A parasite is a living creature that lives on or inside another, feeding on it over time. Parasites are usually much smaller than the host animals they depend on and can live on them for long periods. Some parasites are harmless and others kill their host.

Pea crab

This very small crab is only the size of a pea (of course!) but it is also a crafty parasite. It lives inside shellfish such as clams and mussels, which provide it with food and shelter. Some pea crabs are particularly gross, choosing to make their home in a sea cucumber's bottom.

Tapeworm

These long, flat worms live inside the intestines of animals such as horses, dogs, fish, chickens and human beings. Their heads have suckers or hooks to hang onto their host's gut so that the worm can absorb the food that the host has eaten. The largest tapeworms, found in whales, can be over 25 metres long!

Cowbird

The cowbird of North America doesn't bother to build a nest. It simply lays its eggs in another bird's nest and then flies off. Some birds are tricked by this sneaky scheme and some aren't. They often bring up the cowbird chicks as their own, feeding them constantly but unaware that these parasites will try to push the other chicks out of the nest. Not much gratitude there!

Doh, why did I ever tell him to eat up?

The ked must be fed, mwahahaha!

Sheep ked

This hairy little insect burrows through a sheep's thick fleece so that it can bite it and feed on its blood. The biting irritates the poor sheep, causing it to rub against hard surfaces and damage its fleece. This rascally bug is one of the reasons why farmers dip their sheep in chemical treatments.

Cookiecutter shark

The cookiecutter is small but it's a champion biter, happily taking chunks out of large fish, dolphins, other sharks and even whales. It has a special suction mouth with extra-sharp teeth, which it uses to gouge out a neat chunk of its victim's flesh. They've even been known to attack submarines!

UNWANTED GUESTS: human parasites

Flesh fly

This group of flies feeds on rotting flesh and usually lays their eggs on decaying animal corpses. Occasionally, however, they lay eggs in the open wounds of living mammals, including humans, who then discover that they have maggots crawling around their injuries, looking for dinner. This is why scabs are good!

Guinea worm

A parasite called the guinea worm causes a very unpleasant disease. If a person drinks water that contains fleas carrying the tiny worm larvae, the larvae can develop inside the person's intestines into thin worms up to 80 centimetres long. The worms travel through the body causing severe pain before emerging slowly through a blister in the skin. Thankfully, guinea worm cases are now quite rare.

Can I go back inside? I forgot my hat.

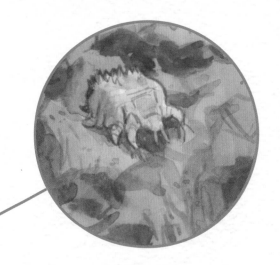

Scabies mite

These teeny-tiny creatures are about a quarter of a millimetre long and they specialise in burrowing into human skin, where they deposit eggs. This usually results in a red rash that is super-itchy. Scabies mites affect over 200 million people worldwide, and they are easily passed on through skin contact. Luckily, they cause no lasting damage.

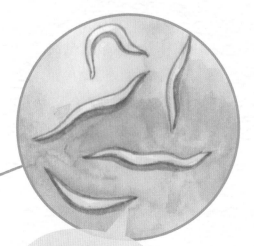

Threadworm

Sometimes called pinworms, these mini parasites are very common in children and can be seen as small white 'threads' in human poo. They get into the body when the worm's microscopic eggs are accidentally eaten, usually from unwashed hands or dirty fingernails. After hatching in the gut, the threadworms emerge from the anus to lay more eggs. This causes itching, which can lead to more eggs on the hands. If you don't want them, don't suck your fingers or bite your nails and remember to wash your hands, you grotty lot!

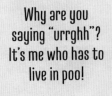

Why are you saying "urrghh"? It's me who has to live in poo!

Botfly

This is one parasite that you really don't want. The large hairy botfly, found mainly in South America, cleverly deposits its eggs on mosquitoes or ticks. When these bloodsuckers bite people, they pass on the botfly larvae. The larvae are giant spiked maggots that burrow under the skin of unlucky human victims, often on the head. They develop under a huge alien-like blister and are hard to extract. Thankfully a rare event, but truly gross!

I'm really nice if you just get to know me.

Body louse

Very similar to its unloved cousin, the head louse, this wingless insect infests humans across the world. They are often picked up when people wear clothes containing lice eggs. When the eggs hatch, the young lice, called nymphs, go in search of blood. Their bites cause itchy rashes and they can spread serious diseases. Apart from that, they're lovely!

Mind control!

Kamikaze horsehair worm

Some parasites can change the behaviour of their host animal by mind control, and the weird kamikaze horsehair worm is an expert. Its larvae are eaten by crickets and inside the insect's body, they develop into thin worms up to 30 centimetres long. But when they want to reproduce they use special nerve-controlling chemicals to make the cricket jump into a pond or river, where it drowns. At this point the worm bores a hole out of the cricket's body and goes off to mate. Clever, albeit gory...

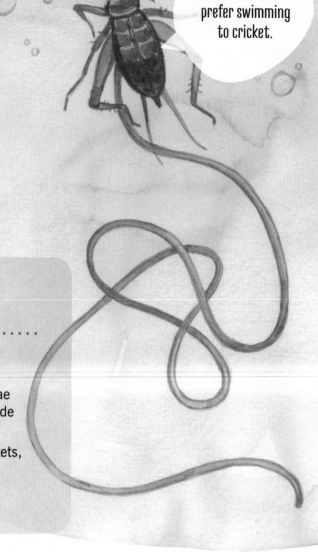

That's better, I prefer swimming to cricket.

HOW A KAMIKAZE WORM GETS INTO A CRICKET

1. An adult worm deposits eggs in a river or pond.

2. The eggs hatch into tiny larvae.

3. The larvae are eaten by the water-dwelling larvae of insects such as mosquitoes, staying alive inside them.

4. The small adult insects are eaten by larger crickets, passing on the worm larvae.

Hurry up, I need a wee.

Ladybird parasite

The ladybird parasite is one of a number of wasp species in the animal kingdom with a sinister power: they can turn their victims into zombies! The female lands on a ladybird and deposits a single egg on its underside. When it hatches, the wasp larva chews through the poor bug's body and then spins a cocoon, trapping the helpless ladybird by fixing it to a plant. The developing wasp is now safely guarded by the zombie ladybird, which warns off predators with its bright spots and ability to produce poison. After a week, the new wasp emerges from its twitching host and flies away.

Riboeira flatworm

This microscopic parasite doesn't control the mind of its frog victims – it controls their bodies, making them grow into gross mutations! Amphibians infested with these minute worms often grow extra legs or sometimes have no legs at all. Frogs with deformed legs have difficulty moving, which means they are easy prey for predatory birds such as herons.

Emerald cockroach wasp

The emerald cockroach wasp (1, below) has a shiny green body and is found across the tropics. It wrestles with a much-larger cockroach and stings it, delivering a shot of mind-controlling chemicals to the brain (2). The cockroach is now the wasp's obedient slave! The wasp fixes a single egg to one of the cockroach's legs before using stones to barricade her mesmerized victim in a nest. When the egg hatches, the larva eats the cockroach alive before finally, as a new wasp, it bursts out of the host's body (3). Grim!

HOW THE FROG-MUTATING FLATWORM SURVIVES

1. The parasite's extremely small eggs attach to a passing snail.

2. The worm larvae hatch and burrow into the snail to grow.

3. The snail releases the larvae into ponds or streams, where they are eaten by tadpoles.

4. As the tadpoles develop into frogs, the worms inside them cause their legs to deform.

5. The frogs are eaten by large birds. The worms reproduce inside the birds and their eggs are released in bird poo, ready for more passing snails...

You WILL do as I say!

COCKROACH VS WASP

1

2

3

Dinner time!

Parasitoid wasp

A large number of wasp species lay their eggs in or on caterpillars. Some deposit up to 70 eggs in the body of the poor caterpillar, which is then eaten alive from the inside by the hungry wasp larvae when they hatch. Eventually lots of new wasps emerge from their shrivelled host which, sadly, will never become a butterfly.

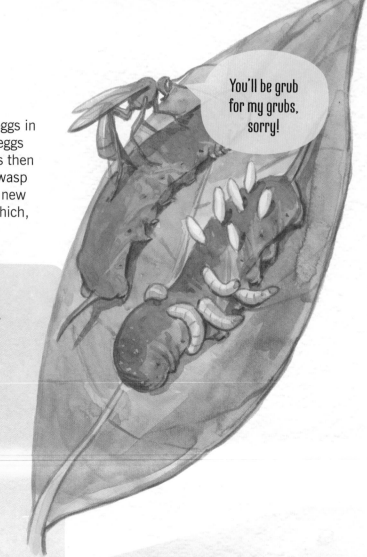

You'll be grub for my grubs, sorry!

PARASITOID WASP FACTS

* These insects are very common: there are over 6000 species in Britain alone!

* Different crafty wasps lay their eggs in ants, flies, moths, spiders, butterflies and bugs such as leafhoppers.

* Some parasitoid wasp larvae have no anus. Their poo would contaminate the host they eat, so they store it in their body.

* A few wasp larvae keep the host alive and only eat part of it.

* Some parasitoid wasps lay their eggs in other parasitoid wasps!

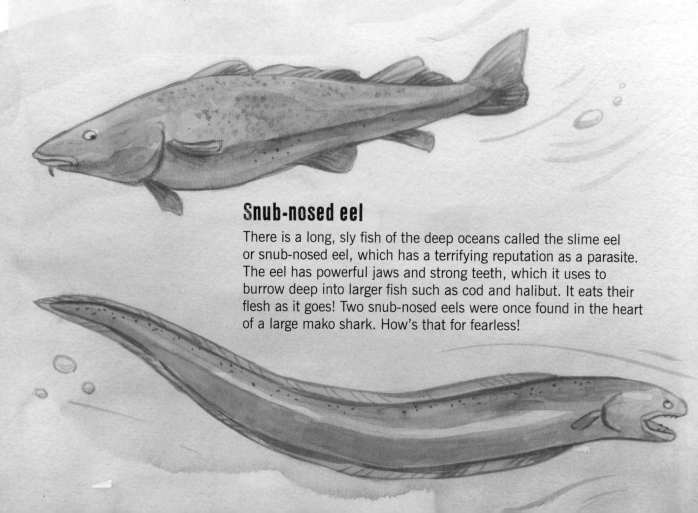

Snub-nosed eel

There is a long, sly fish of the deep oceans called the slime eel or snub-nosed eel, which has a terrifying reputation as a parasite. The eel has powerful jaws and strong teeth, which it uses to burrow deep into larger fish such as cod and halibut. It eats their flesh as it goes! Two snub-nosed eels were once found in the heart of a large mako shark. How's that for fearless!

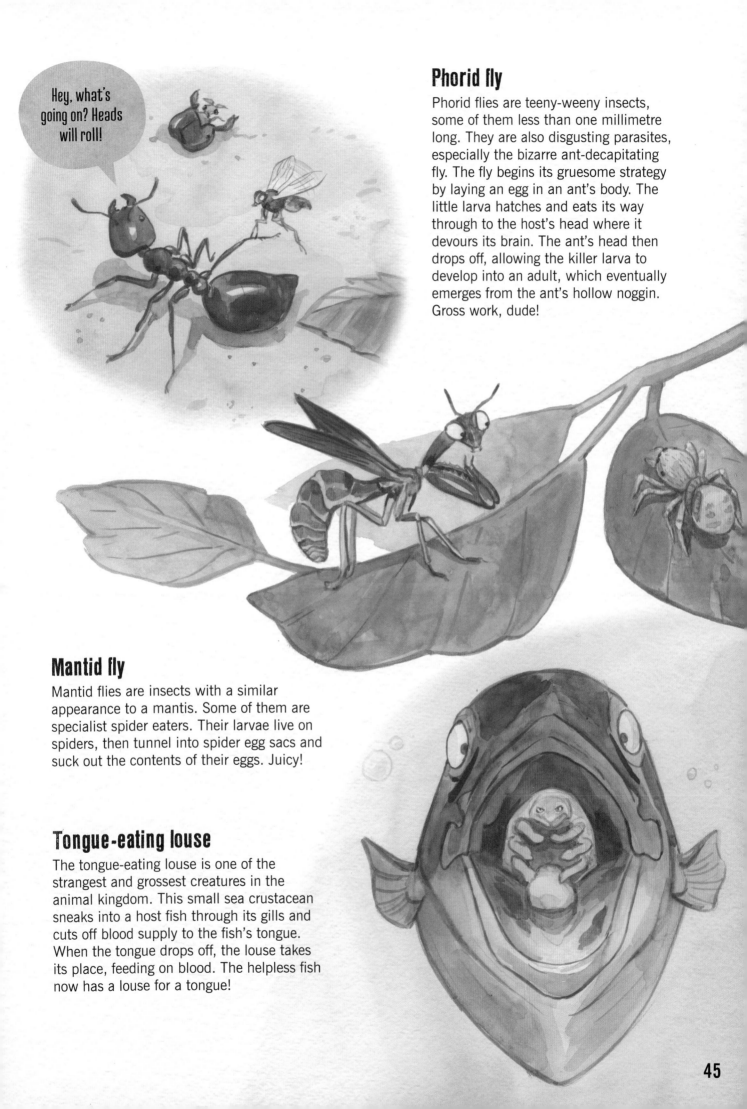

Hey, what's going on? Heads will roll!

Phorid fly

Phorid flies are teeny-weeny insects, some of them less than one millimetre long. They are also disgusting parasites, especially the bizarre ant-decapitating fly. The fly begins its gruesome strategy by laying an egg in an ant's body. The little larva hatches and eats its way through to the host's head where it devours its brain. The ant's head then drops off, allowing the killer larva to develop into an adult, which eventually emerges from the ant's hollow noggin. Gross work, dude!

Mantid fly

Mantid flies are insects with a similar appearance to a mantis. Some of them are specialist spider eaters. Their larvae live on spiders, then tunnel into spider egg sacs and suck out the contents of their eggs. Juicy!

Tongue-eating louse

The tongue-eating louse is one of the strangest and grossest creatures in the animal kingdom. This small sea crustacean sneaks into a host fish through its gills and cuts off blood supply to the fish's tongue. When the tongue drops off, the louse takes its place, feeding on blood. The helpless fish now has a louse for a tongue!

I know, aren't I gorgeous?!

We love wee!
Red deer
Male red deer looking for females to mate with have a cunning plan. They find a shallow dip in the ground, pee in it, then roll around in the muddy, stinky gloop they've created. Amazingly, this seems to work! Their urine contains potent chemicals called pheromones, which female deer find attractive.

STINKY!: Animals that pong

TOP PIDDLE FACT
Fin whales urinate about 970 litres a day on average. That's enough to fill 5½ bathtubs!

Some smells are really gross, and wild animals have all kinds of whiffy ways of creating them. They are experts at using special stench glands to produce oily gloop that reeks. They also spray yucky urine, fire beastly bottom burps, and produce mountains of pongy poo and puke. Nature is smelly, but animals always make their stinks for a reason!

Squirrel monkey
Squirrel monkeys are small, busy, tree-dwelling primates found across South and Central America. Like other monkeys, they have an interesting way to communicate with each other, called urine washing. They pee on their hands and feet and then spread the urine on their bodies. This wee-wash may also help to keep them cool in the steamy hot jungle.

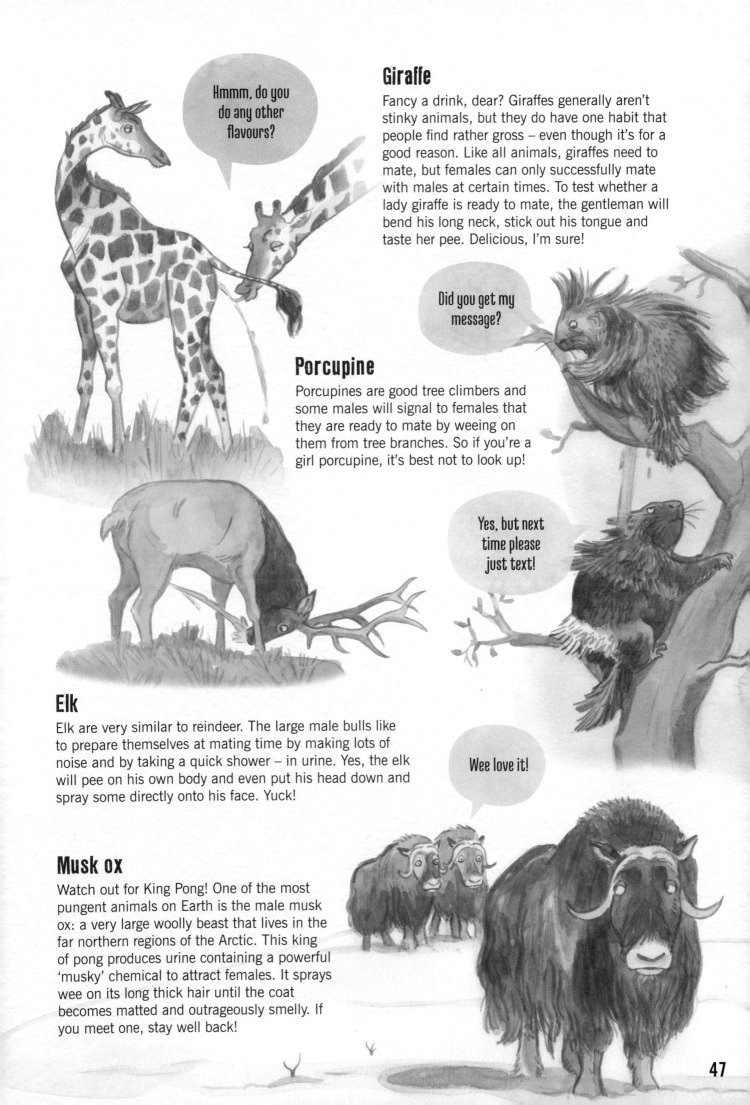

Giraffe

Fancy a drink, dear? Giraffes generally aren't stinky animals, but they do have one habit that people find rather gross – even though it's for a good reason. Like all animals, giraffes need to mate, but females can only successfully mate with males at certain times. To test whether a lady giraffe is ready to mate, the gentleman will bend his long neck, stick out his tongue and taste her pee. Delicious, I'm sure!

Porcupine

Porcupines are good tree climbers and some males will signal to females that they are ready to mate by weeing on them from tree branches. So if you're a girl porcupine, it's best not to look up!

Elk

Elk are very similar to reindeer. The large male bulls like to prepare themselves at mating time by making lots of noise and by taking a quick shower – in urine. Yes, the elk will pee on his own body and even put his head down and spray some directly onto his face. Yuck!

Musk ox

Watch out for King Pong! One of the most pungent animals on Earth is the male musk ox: a very large woolly beast that lives in the far northern regions of the Arctic. This king of pong produces urine containing a powerful 'musky' chemical to attract females. It sprays wee on its long thick hair until the coat becomes matted and outrageously smelly. If you meet one, stay well back!

Watch out!

It's just the way I roll, you know?

Poo will do!

Chinstrap penguin

These penguins of the far south are clever with poo. When their chicks hatch they must protect them from predators, so they try to leave the nest as little as possible. But they don't want stinky droppings around their young, so when they need the loo they bend over, point their rear end away and shoot it out at high power. Yes, chinstrap penguins have projectile poo!

Minotaur beetle

The clever minotaur beetle uses stinky poo as a nursery! This insect spends most of its time in search of sheep or rabbit poo. When found, the dung lump is buried and the female lays an egg in it. Upon hatching, the beetle larva is protected by poo and also has something to eat. Bonus!

Wombat

Wombat poo is unique in the whole animal kingdom: it is cube-shaped. Scientists think one of the reasons they do this cubic doo-doo is to stop it rolling away when they leave piles of poo lying around to mark their territories. These are building blocks you don't want to play with!

Ouch!

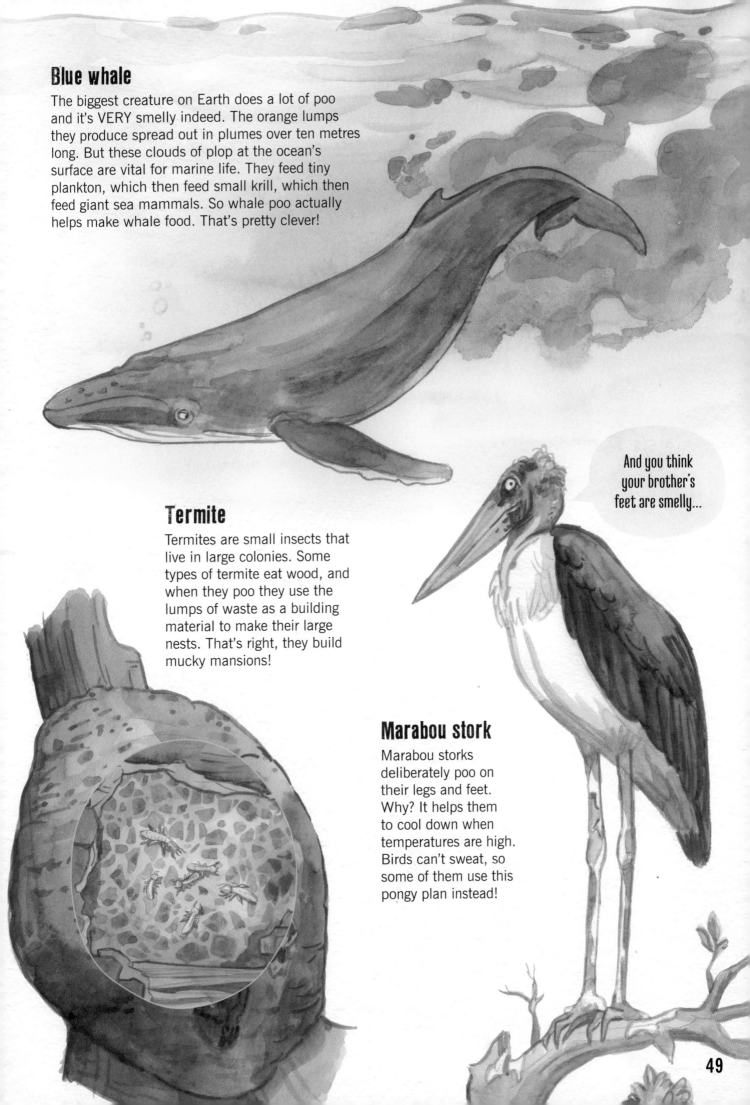

Blue whale

The biggest creature on Earth does a lot of poo and it's VERY smelly indeed. The orange lumps they produce spread out in plumes over ten metres long. But these clouds of plop at the ocean's surface are vital for marine life. They feed tiny plankton, which then feed small krill, which then feed giant sea mammals. So whale poo actually helps make whale food. That's pretty clever!

Termite

Termites are small insects that live in large colonies. Some types of termite eat wood, and when they poo they use the lumps of waste as a building material to make their large nests. That's right, they build mucky mansions!

And you think your brother's feet are smelly...

Marabou stork

Marabou storks deliberately poo on their legs and feet. Why? It helps them to cool down when temperatures are high. Birds can't sweat, so some of them use this pongy plan instead!

Stay back!

Hoopoe

The hoopoe of Europe and Asia is the crested punk of the bird world with a wonderful scientific name: *Upupa epops*. However, if you see a hoopoe nest, don't get too close. For a start, the female coats her feathers in a liquid that smells like rotting flesh. As if that wasn't gross enough, her chicks are capable of squirting liquid faeces at intruders. Yes, they are armed with poo guns!

Stink badger

The tigers on the large island of Sumatra are not scared of much, but one animal they keep well away from is the stink badger. It's quite small and isn't actually a badger, but it has a bottom loaded with a weapons-grade pong. When threatened, the stink badger can squirt a reeking yellow liquid out of special anal glands. This is so powerful and revolting that even the biggest predators steer clear.

BEWARE THE STINK BADGER'S EVEN STINKIER COUSIN: THE SKUNK

Skunks are found in North America and are legendary for their smelly defence…

- Skunks can spray a noxious chemical up to 3 metres.
- The smell is sometimes described as a mixture of rotten eggs, old wee and burnt rubber.
- Skunk spray is flammable.
- The smell is incredibly hard to get rid of.

Free scent sample, sir?

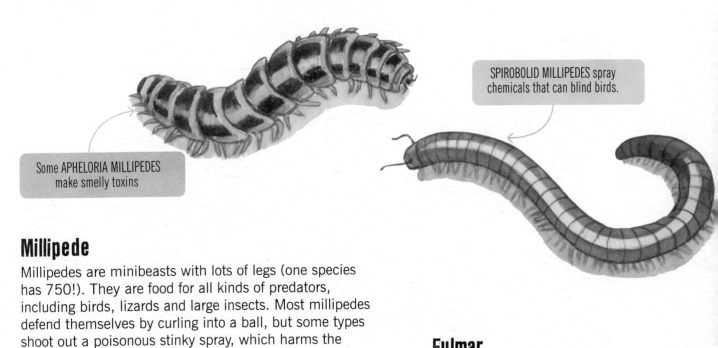

Some APHELORIA MILLIPEDES make smelly toxins

SPIROBOLID MILLIPEDES spray chemicals that can blind birds.

Millipede

Millipedes are minibeasts with lots of legs (one species has 750!). They are food for all kinds of predators, including birds, lizards and large insects. Most millipedes defend themselves by curling into a ball, but some types shoot out a poisonous stinky spray, which harms the attacker's eyes and skin.

Fulmar

Fulmars are seabirds that nest on cliffs and islands. Their plump babies are sometimes approached by predators looking for an easy meal, but if an attacker gets too near then it may get coated in stinky chick sick. The young birds vomit foul-smelling stomach oil, which sticks to birds' feathers. Amazingly, the chicks are precision pukers and can aim spew from the day they hatch! It may sound gross but, for the birds, it can be a life-saver.

Turkey vulture

The turkey vulture has a gross trick up its sleeve if attacked. It vomits up extra-whiffy half-digested meat, creating such a stench that predators retreat. This yucky turkey barf is also coated in burning stomach acid. That's enough to put anything off its dinner…

DANGER: gas attack!

Cow

It seems like cows do nothing but stand in a field, munching grass. But chances are that they are sneakily burping and farting away too. The bad news is that their gassy outgoings account for about 10 per cent of all greenhouse gases, which contribute to global warming. One of these is the explosive gas methane. In Germany in 2014, a build-up of methane from cows exploded, blowing the roof off a cowshed!

Sea lion

According to the head zookeeper at San Diego Zoo in the USA, sea lions do the smelliest farts of all. They eat a diet of fish and squid, so their trumps are both foul and fishy. What's more, they really don't care who is around when they blow off. You've been warned!

Beaded lacewing

Silent but deadly! Beaded lacewings are insects with killer farts. They deposit their eggs in termite nests and when the larvae hatch out, they feed on the termites. And they catch them by using a death fart! Scientists observed the lethal maggots waving their rear ends and stunning termites before eating them. It is thought that the larvae's fatal farts contain toxic chemicals strong enough to slay their prey. Nasty!

Hippo

You should never stand behind a hippo. For a start, it might sit on you and since they can weigh over 1.5 tonnes, that's bad news. But a hippo also does some really disgusting things with its rear end. It produces enormous thundering farts that are usually accompanied by a gush of liquid poo, sent spattering in all directions by the hippo flapping its little tail. If it happens, just run!

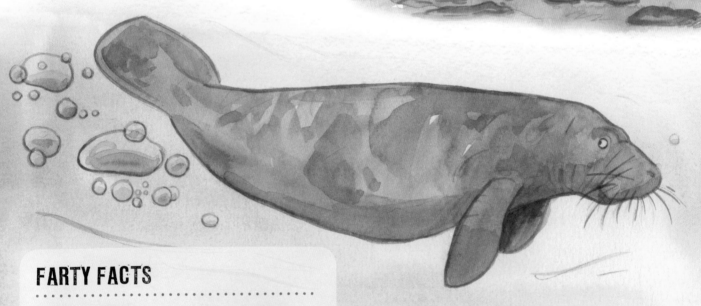

FARTY FACTS

ANIMALS THAT DON'T FART

* Birds
* Sloths
* Goldfish
* Sea anemones
* Clams

BIG TOOTERS

* Horses
* Rhinos
* Elephants
* Zebras
* Whales
* Termites

Manatee

Manatees are large sea mammals, like overinflated seals. But unlike seals, they feed on plants rather than fish. These sea cows, as they are sometimes called, use farts to control their swimming. Holding in farts gives them buoyancy so they float, and letting rip helps them to dive. It's pump propulsion!

WACKY!: Animals that are very strange and gross

The diversity of nature is staggering. There are simply millions of different types of animals found across our planet. Some are big, some are tiny, some are dangerous, some are cuddly – and some are very odd indeed. Here's a look at a few of the stranger organisms with a touch of the gross about them.

Brainless creatures

Jellyfish

The jellyfish is a weird wonder of the oceans. It has no head, no brain, no heart, no blood and no bones, but it does have a mouth. Despite being 95 per cent water, the largest ones are over 2 metres across and some have stinging tentacles that can kill. Others travel in swarms of thousands and certain species eat fish and crabs.

Starfish

Starfish sneak around the sea floor looking for food. If they find a juicy oyster or snail they push their stomach out of their mouth to start digesting it. They have no brain, so they are not deep thinkers, but they do have between 5 and 50 arms (with eyes on the end) and they can grow a new limb if one is bitten off by a hungry predator. Oh, and despite their name, they're not fish!

I always wanted to be a rock star!

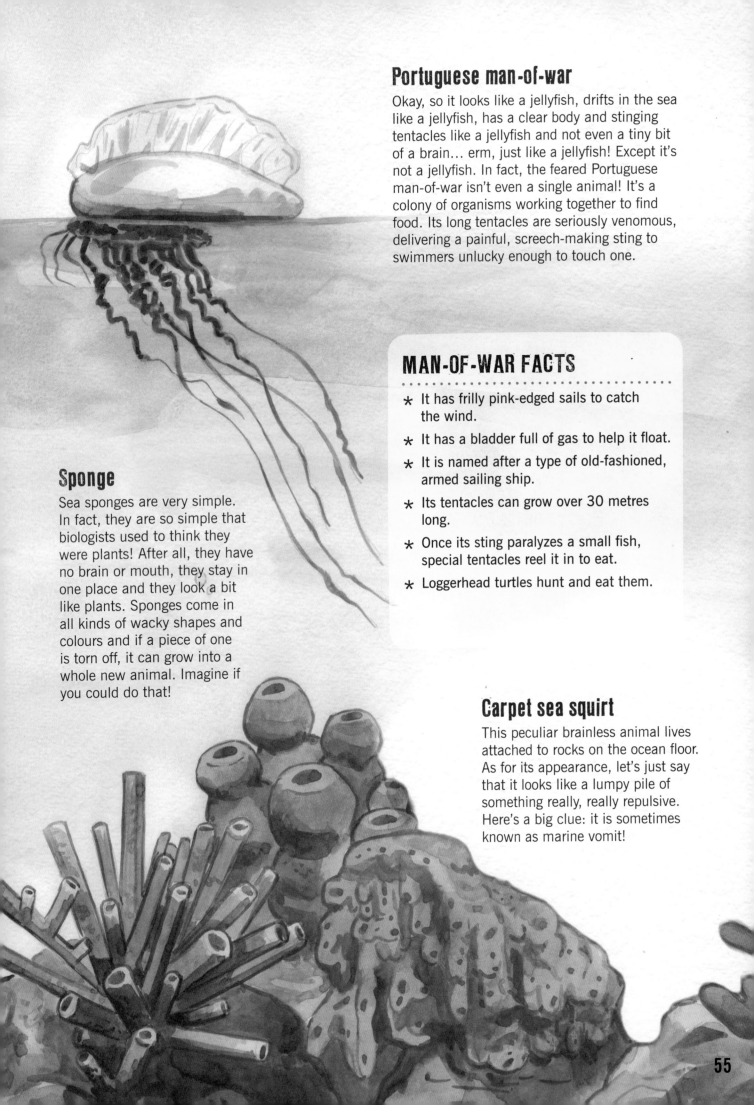

Portuguese man-of-war

Okay, so it looks like a jellyfish, drifts in the sea like a jellyfish, has a clear body and stinging tentacles like a jellyfish and not even a tiny bit of a brain... erm, just like a jellyfish! Except it's not a jellyfish. In fact, the feared Portuguese man-of-war isn't even a single animal! It's a colony of organisms working together to find food. Its long tentacles are seriously venomous, delivering a painful, screech-making sting to swimmers unlucky enough to touch one.

MAN-OF-WAR FACTS

* It has frilly pink-edged sails to catch the wind.
* It has a bladder full of gas to help it float.
* It is named after a type of old-fashioned, armed sailing ship.
* Its tentacles can grow over 30 metres long.
* Once its sting paralyzes a small fish, special tentacles reel it in to eat.
* Loggerhead turtles hunt and eat them.

Sponge

Sea sponges are very simple. In fact, they are so simple that biologists used to think they were plants! After all, they have no brain or mouth, they stay in one place and they look a bit like plants. Sponges come in all kinds of wacky shapes and colours and if a piece of one is torn off, it can grow into a whole new animal. Imagine if you could do that!

Carpet sea squirt

This peculiar brainless animal lives attached to rocks on the ocean floor. As for its appearance, let's just say that it looks like a lumpy pile of something really, really repulsive. Here's a big clue: it is sometimes known as marine vomit!

Slimy creatures

Slug

Slugs move around on a thin layer of slime. The goo they produce helps their legless bodies to travel and to climb, but it can also do much more. It can protect them from predators and it helps them to communicate – yes, slugs can 'read' slime! They can also dangle from a thread of mucus as a quick means of escape.

Goliath tigerfish

Many fish, including the Goliath tigerfish, 'wear' a layer of slime on their bodies. This slippery coat protects its wearer against infection and blood-sucking parasites. It's also one of the reasons why it's very hard to hold a fish!

Being a ninja isn't as much fun as I'd hoped.

Hagfish

Hagfish are peculiar slime specialists of the deep. They look like eels and use their long, snaky bodies to burrow into the remains of dead marine animals on the sea bed and then eat their way out! If they are attacked by a big bully fish such as a shark, they can spurt around a litre of goo out of their bodies. This can clog up a shark's gills, choking it and sending it away confused and hungry.

Nudibranch

Nudibranchs are a group of sea slugs with amazing brightly coloured bodies that warn off predators. They have a toxic way of defending themselves, and how they get it is remarkable: they steal from their prey. A nudibranch loves nothing better than to lunch on a passing jellyfish, stings and all. It uses special slug slime to disarm the stingers and then cleverly stores them in its own body to fire at any passing attackers. Mucus murder!

Parrotfish

Parrotfish are wacky and gross for a few reasons. First, they have heads like parrots, complete with a beaky mouth. Second, they bite off and swallow lumps of hard coral, which causes them to poo out sand. And third, some types of parrotfish make a kind of mucus tent to sleep in at night! This is thought to protect them from predators and blood-sucking sea parasites.

Hey, 'snot bad in here!

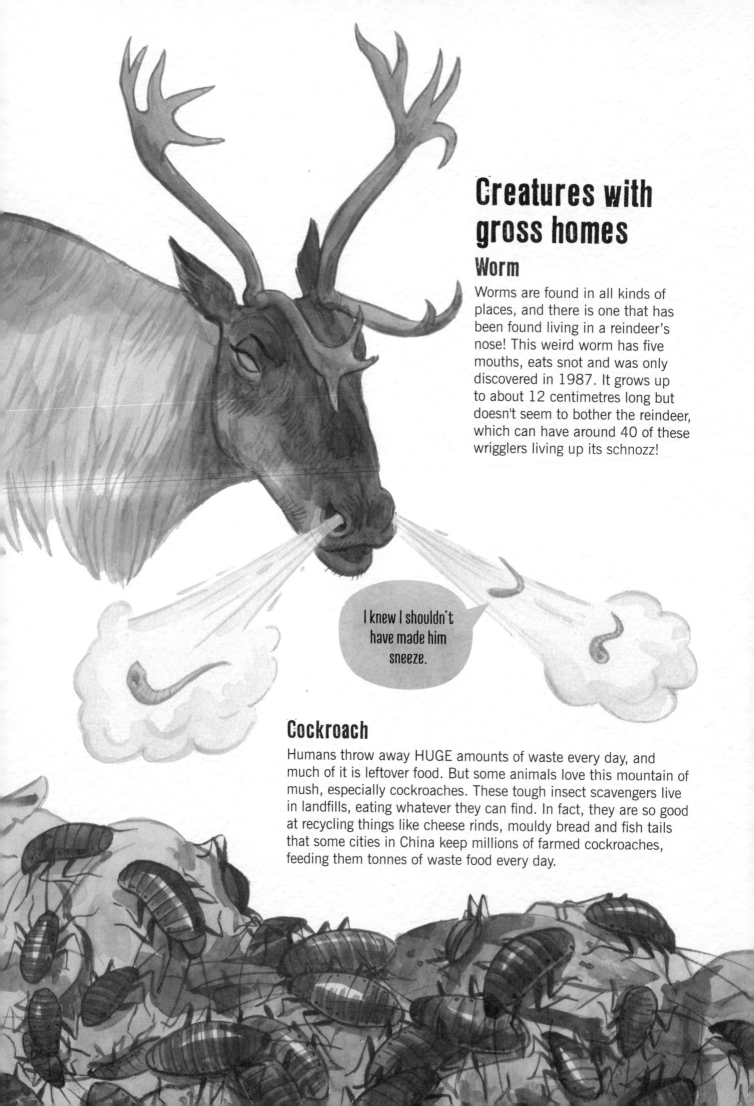

Creatures with gross homes

Worm

Worms are found in all kinds of places, and there is one that has been found living in a reindeer's nose! This weird worm has five mouths, eats snot and was only discovered in 1987. It grows up to about 12 centimetres long but doesn't seem to bother the reindeer, which can have around 40 of these wrigglers living up its schnozz!

I knew I shouldn't have made him sneeze.

Cockroach

Humans throw away HUGE amounts of waste every day, and much of it is leftover food. But some animals love this mountain of mush, especially cockroaches. These tough insect scavengers live in landfills, eating whatever they can find. In fact, they are so good at recycling things like cheese rinds, mouldy bread and fish tails that some cities in China keep millions of farmed cockroaches, feeding them tonnes of waste food every day.

Rat

Rats are great survivors, capable of living in all kinds of environments. Lots of them live in drains and sewers, where they can move around out of sight. They're not fussy about sewage, either. Rats are also excellent swimmers and can wriggle up toilets into houses in search of food and shelter. So, keep the lid down!

Pearlfish

The pearlfish is long and thin, like an eel – the perfect shape for worming into small holes. And what kind of hole is just right, offering shelter from predators? A sea cucumber's bottom, that's what! Yes, this funny fish lives part of its life in the bum of another sea creature. In fact, as many as 16 pearlfish can hide in a single anus. You could call it the house at poo corner...

Do you mind? I'm having a piddle.

Welcome to life at the bottom!

Frog

Elephants are big animals, so they do big poos. I mean REALLY big poos, adding up to around 50 kilograms a day! In Sri Lanka, some frogs have found that these large slimy heaps make a good place in which to spend their time. The dung helps keep the frogs' skin moist and the piles make an excellent, if smelly, place to hide from predators such as large birds.

This place is a dump.

Even more gross and wacky animals

Drongo

The black drongo, which lives in South Asia, will sometimes land on an ants' nest and let the ants crawl over its body. Many other birds also engage in 'anting', but experts are not sure why they do it. Some argue that the birds are bathing in the ants' acid to help get rid of parasites like mites. Other people say it's a way to make the ants easier to eat. It's a mystery!

I know why I do it, but I'm not telling. Ha!

Green iguana

The green iguana is a big South American lizard, growing up to 1.5 metres long. It has some handy defences against predators such as hawks, cats and snakes. There are spines along its back, it boasts a nasty bite and can give attackers a sharp whack across the face with its heavy tail. But if the tail is grabbed the iguana simply detaches it and runs off. The tail continues to wriggle, confusing the predator, while the crafty lizard escapes to grow a new one.

Frog

Frogs like water, but the water-holding frog of Australia is often faced with long, hot, dry summers. So, during the rainy season it buries itself deep in gloopy mud and then waits a whole year for the next time the ground is squelchy. The frog holds water in its body during this long burial and lives in a bubble of old skin and mucus, which it later eats. Well, you'd be hungry too, after a year in the mud!

Brown bear

Brown bears love eating fish and they are experts at catching salmon in rivers. But in Canada and Alaska, at the end of the summer there are often so many salmon swimming up shallow rivers to spawn that the local bears can afford to be choosy. They eat only the best bits of each fish, and for them that's the brain, eggs and skin.

I've got loads of brains. In my tum, that is!

Toad

In Germany in 2005, hundreds of toads started bursting for no obvious reason. One minute they were hopping along, minding their own business, then their guts splattered everywhere and the poor toads were goners. The exploding toads were the result of sneaky crows pecking out the toads' livers. This caused the poor amphibians to swell and then pop, leaving a gory mess. Gross indeed!

Looks like I'm going to go out with a bang...

I really am bursting for the loo!

Scorpion

Scorpions are not to be messed with. The stingers on their tails can inject paralysing venom into their prey. However, one particular type of scorpion has a tail that can drop off as a defence against predators. What happens next is incredibly gross. Dropping its tail means that the scorpion no longer has an anus and therefore can't poo. As it eats, its body gradually fills with poo until it dies. What a way to go (or not go, really)!

TOTALLY GROSS!

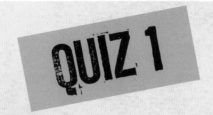

1. Which pink wobbly creature eats the bodies of dead whales?
a) Sea pig
b) Portuguese man-of-war
c) Goblin shark
d) Kobadai

2. Sticky goo from which animal's bottom was once used to flavour ice cream?
a) Moose
b) Beaver
c) Gharial
d) Opossum

3. What does the horned lizard do when attacked?
a) Vomits
b) Sprays stinky fluid
c) Explodes
d) Squirts blood out of its eyes

4. Which animal loves to roll around in its own vomit?
a) Warthog
b) Fulmar
c) Rat
d) Hyena

5. Which animal was once observed coming out of a toad's bottom alive?
a) Snake
b) Dung beetle
c) Tapeworm
d) Newt

6. What part of a giraffe does the oxpecker bird like to snack on?
a) Toenails
b) Snot and earwax
c) Hair and horns
d) Poo

7. Which babies eat their mother if she dies?
a) Scorpions
b) Earwigs
c) Chimpanzees
d) Owls

8. Which predator turns its victims into liquid so it can drink them?
a) Yeti crab
b) Vampire bat
c) Assassin bug
d) Sexton beetle

9. Tapeworms are parasites that live in the guts of host animals. How long can they grow?
a) 4m
b) 18m
c) 25m
d) 97m

10. What does a male elk do to attract a mate?
a) Rolls in dead bodies
b) Farts yellow gas
c) Poos on its feet
d) Wees on its head

TOTALLY GROSS!

1. Which creature sometimes buries its head in a victim's skin when feeding on blood?
a) Flea
b) Mosquito
c) Tick
d) Bedbug

2. Where do threadworms emerge from their host's body?
a) Anus
b) Mouth
c) Skin
d) Nose

3. The phorid fly is a parasite of ants. What happens to an ant that has a phorid fly larva inside?
a) It grows extra legs
b) Its head falls off
c) It can't move
d) It jumps into water

4. How does a beaded lacewing disable termites?
a) Bites their legs off
b) With a giant sting
c) Using hypnotism
d) With toxic farts

5. Which animal has no head, no brain, no bones and no blood?
a) Squid
b) Jellyfish
c) Sea slug
d) Millipede

6. Which of these is a type of gross-looking sea slug?
a) Nudibranch
b) Blobneck
c) Slimehead
d) Nakibum

7. When a crow pecks out a toad's liver, what happens to the toad?
a) It dies on the spot
b) It goes blind
c) It turns purple
d) It later explodes

8. Which 25-centimetre-long yellow animal do some people eat?
a) Golden stick insect
b) Melon fish
c) Banana slug
d) Lemon worm

9. Which male animal tastes its partner's urine to see if she's ready to reproduce?
a) Howler monkey
b) Red deer
c) Giraffe
d) Panda

10. What does a female octopus sometimes do to a male after mating?
a) Pulls an arm off
b) Pokes him in the eye
c) Steals his food
d) Eats him

Index

QUIZ ANSWERS

QUIZ 1: 1a 2b 3d 4d 5a 6b 7b 8c 9c 10d **QUIZ 2:** 1c 2a 3b 4d 5b 6a 7d 8c 9c 10d